INTERNATIONAL CHRISTIAN
GRADUATE UNIVERSITY

Welcome Retirement

WELCOME RETIREMENT

Elmer Otte

EDITOR
Harold Belgum

Publishing House
St. Louis

To Margaret, who often suffers doubts similar
to those of any other wife of any other practicing optimist—especially one who indulges
in self-lectures such as this—however
provable they may be.

Concordia Publishing House, St. Louis, Missouri

Copyright © 1974 Concordia Publishing House
Library of Congress Catalog Card No. 73-11880
ISBN 0-570-06766-9

A Few Words from the Author . . .

Retirement is a reality coming finally to most workers in life's vineyard.

You are going to be retired sometime. Either that will happen when you want it to or when "they" make it happen.

You will gain personal freedom and the wonderful gift of free time to use just as you wish.

You will lose something too: your importance, perhaps; your role in the work community and with lifelong job associates. You will cease to have a paycheck, though this may be partially replaced by some more modest retirement income.

How you respond to these changes which retirement will surely bring makes all the difference. Pensions are not enough. Frequently leisure is too much time—with too little planned for its enjoyment or employment.

The kind of retirement you can expect depends on your attitudes—his *and* hers. How you will enjoy retirement may depend in large measure on what you do now to prepare for that golden time. How much will you do to rehearse for it beforehand?

Elmer Otte
1974

CONTENTS

CHAPTER 1

Almost Everybody Retires — Sometime

Many economists — and many laymen — feel there's something almost sinfully wasteful about forcing people to retire at age 65, or at any other age which may be arbitrarily set for workers in our society. Actually that age limit shows signs of being lowered further by companies, in labor organizations, and within governmental bodies.

We find that in many European countries early retirement is either available or required, often at ages as low as 55, 58, or 60.

Can Leisure Be Redistributed?

There is a study, by one of the world organizations concerned with labor, which investigates the redistribution of leisure throughout the worker's lifetime rather than saving it all as an uncertain gift for the weary end of a hardworking lifetime.

Avoid Retirement Surprises

Evidence shows that retirement is better if you plan for it. Case after case is reported where men found themselves delivered into retirement by serious illness which required long convalescence and complete work stoppage. Or they were bedeviled by boring jobs and sought retirement as early as 55 or 58 only to find that pensions won't buy daily usefulness and nightly contentment. Too often workers find that it takes more than "being free" from work and job pressures to dispel boredom, frustration, lonely and empty days.

Not many vacation trips work successfully if they are no better planned than jumping into the family car and driving off in all directions without preplanned and interesting goals.

It has been said that good retirement does not arrive by special delivery. Nor does it come as a guarantee with Social Security or pensions. There are a number of specific tasks you must do for yourself before retirement can be as good as it might. There are certain decisions *you* must make.

Who makes these decisions in your family? How's your communication level? Being able to talk over the alternatives you will face when you retire—together—is absolutely essential so that these questions: When will you retire? What will you do? and Where will you live? can be resolved to satisfy both retirement partners.

It may be elementary, but in most families it is the husband and father who is considered to be retiring. Often there is also a working wife. Her retirement may not mesh with his. Beyond this, it's the man who retires and gives up familiar lifetime roles. Not so with his wife. She has homemaking and other wifely roles to play. But now she gets a new "helper." In many cases that's like having a new "child" around the house, but too often one who thinks he's the boss. It may be trite but it's true. She gets less than half the income and more than twice the husband. Not that she wishes him elsewhere—or otherwise. Wives are really great at cautioning husbands about killing themselves by working too hard. And they mean it! But they are just as sincere (even if it comes after the fact) about not wanting him underfoot, at home, all day, every day.

Communications Travel Both Ways

You bet there's a lot of communication needed and some thoughtful decisions to be made together!

Don't let your retirement come as a "surprise party," especially if this can be avoided. Stay involved in the decision about when you will retire. You may think such decisions belong only to employers or are dictated by pension fund requirements or Social Security jurisdictions. Certainly these have a bearing. But if you plan ahead you will know beforehand when you *might* retire or when you would *like* to retire. You will know when you *can* retire and when you *will* retire.

Two different friends were expecting to retire in six and nine months respectively. But they had their psychological rugs pulled out from under one day in surprise early retirement pronouncements.

Both had had recent poor health records. In both cases the employers commiserated that these "premature" moves were actually being made to help protect the remaining health of such valued and respected employees. Concern was expressed about conserving their remaining health and protecting their personal welfare.

In both cases there was a big fuss. Prides had been punctured — masculine pride, about a matter of a few months. Both of these near-45-year employees tainted a part of their life's success imagery by maligning the company to anyone who would listen.

Later changes in the company's structure proved that both had indeed been lucky to have been "saved" beforehand.

Our only point is the caution that these twin experiences suggest. Keep your own retirement options open so that unexpected shuffling won't matter too much. Expect retirement and accept it graciously.

It is not unlawful, nor is it being disloyal to their firms or jobs, for the workers of the world to keep their options open about how they will live their lives—especially that part of living which we call "the reward of retirement."

Pick Your Own Crowning Reward

You've got to decide what you want from your retirement. It may help to face the fact now that you will both probably live a large part of your lifetime as retired persons—from 15 to 30 years or more!

What would you most like to do with so much wonderful free time?

Dig back into your childhood, into former school interests or into hobbies and other extracurricular activities to find those very special and important things you still want to do.

Retirement is probably an inadequate word because it indicates, most often erroneously, that this is the end for the worker. So much better if you will look ahead as early as you can to "the opportunity" which retirement will bring you—to create still one more part-time career activity or avocational interest which you can turn into still one more "lifetime." And make this the really important one—for you.

Employee-benefit directors and the people at Social Security encourage many employed persons to consider retiring at age 62 instead of waiting until 65. There are lots of reasons for this. You should have more vitality and excitement left in your psychic system at this younger age. And, if you wish to "jump ship" a little earlier, there's a chance that you'll still grab hold of "one more brass ring" for the excitement of doing something just for the fun of it—or for the love you can bring to some of life's neighbors or even for picking up a little new money.

Expect "to Live" Even in Retirement

Actually gerontology experts report that prepared retirees live longer, happier retirement lives. Look ahead toward the opportunity of your retirement; do some specific things to prepare for that wonderfully golden gift and you'll stand a better chance of skipping over what geriatric experts call the "hurdle of age 66." March on to new worlds to conquer and to new joys you can still find.

It's sad to see responsible husbands and fathers, hard workers, come home after their retirement party to sit around, to stare idly, feeling cheated of their former importance. It is far better to grab control of this problem in advance, to turn it into another kind of opportunity.

There's. a great justice in the concept of thinking of retirement as a reward. But rewards must be collected by the winner, and most often this needs to be done in person. There's little that's automatic about a successful retirement. But we can guarantee that you will have the satisfying joy of a fulfilling retirement if you take some steps in advance.

What kind of role do you want to play during those remaining "living" years?

Remember that you *are* going to be retired. Almost everyone arrives there sometime. Welcome your retirement and turn it into a special reward!

Retirement Preparation Exercises

- Write a simple statement—your plan for retirement.
- Take a few specific steps to decide when you will retire.
- List three or more things you should do to prepare.
- Consider retiring at age 62; would you like to?
- Write down some of the rewards you expect from retirement.

CHAPTER 2

The Problem of Money
in Retirement

Retirement is not all reward in the fearful minds of many families approaching that time of life. Always listed among the top fears connected with approaching retirement is the matter of money. Actually it's not just the concern about having enough money for its own sake but also because people have the mistaken view that money will also bring them good health. Losing one's health is one of our biggest fears, but it's difficult to understand how money will assure better health.

More than Only Money

Thinking that money is the key to good retirement is such a sad fallacy! One has only to visit luxuriant retirement paradises to quickly sense how unsatisfactory money alone can be to dispel boredom and loneliness if these have not been otherwise provided for in planning and practice.

We know good friends and neighbors who retired with more than enough money to live on — and to leave behind! And yet we see a frantic fiddling to fill the empty days, making extra trips, going out to eat more often, killing time rather than harnessing it to some worthwhileness. We are speaking here of a "successful" retiree who "put his power mower up on blocks" because pushing around the old hand mower used up more of his free time.

Poor Time for Money Surprises

We know another friend whose abrupt health-changes forced an earlier retirement at a down-time in the stock market. His new health concerns were a new psychological burden, and diminished retirement reserves added unneeded concern at a wrong time.

There's a wonderfully hopeful word of warning we have been asked to share. It comes from a lady who lived in prewar Europe, as a girl and later as an inmate in a concentration camp. She was an intellectual, a doctor — and Jewish. The fact that she lived at all beyond those times is some kind of miracle. She became a psychiatrist later and witnessed in her American practice so much unnecessary anxiety. Too often this centered on the lack of money or on the fear of losing it. She asked me to tell you a few simple thoughts based on her observations and experiences. In our society, according to this wise woman, people do not generally go hungry. Barring unforeseen plagues and pestilence, there will always be enough to eat and no one will starve. She said this knowledge should relieve people from the obsessive fear of going hungry.

This may strike many of you as an unreal concept, but it gets down to basic realities of an important retirement fear. It's difficult in our society to keep money in focus. Money is necessary to keep our wheels turning as smoothly as possible. There are other important retirement realities about money.

Less Money — Lessened Needs

When you retire you will almost certainly have less income than you had while you were working. You usually also begin having lessened appetites and decreasing energies so that it's possible to manage on less. Most retired couples will assure you that it's natural and necessary to learn to live on less. Retired people generally expect to

15

live somewhat simpler lives. And blessed are those spouses who can learn this lesson without too much self-pitying trauma about their altered circumstances.

Assets Are Fine — Cash Flow Is Better

The way to look at the problem of money in retirement is to consider the need for income rather than to sit around adding up one's assets. Assets must produce income for living, or they won't be doing anybody much good. Anybody, that is, except perhaps the psychiatrists of another generation!

You may ask what psychiatry has to do with retirement money. We have it on official authority from practicing psychiatrists that an abnormal number of their patients have among their various hang-ups the extra guilt burden of possessing money they didn't have to work for. "Dad always worked hard and seemed to have so little time to enjoy life. He and Mom scrimped and saved and left it for us kids. Why couldn't they have enjoyed it themselves?" Often too large an inheritance is left to families still too young and immature.

I'm sure you'll nod your head and say, "That's a problem I'd like to be burdened with." Several successful "problem doctors" assure us that it's better for you to feel poor and struggling than to get unexpectedly "rich."

Expect to Earn Some New Money

Who said you're never going to make any new money during the rest of your lifetime? As a matter of fact, it's a good idea if you're just a little short of what you think you need — or what you'd really like to have for living in retirement. That's a good way to help generate your imagination in search of hidden hobbies and avocational powers. It can be through this pursuit that you are going to fill your remaining days with activities and excitement and a little

16

inevitable new income. The last shall be sweeter than the first because now the heat's off. It's extra and unexpected, and it helps psychologically to insure your independence.

We have several delightful case histories of two families from two different economic backgrounds who decided near age 60 to begin to live as if they were already retired. Don't turn away from this kind of childlike problem-solving. Listen to what it did to a plant worker on the one hand and to a physician on the other. The worker and his wife spent the two years prior to 62 living as if they were already retired. He worked and earned the same, but they began to curtail some costs and to adjust others. They found ways to replace budget-damaging surprises through planned entertainment with compatible companions, through cultivating simpler tastes, and adhering to more amenable budgets. True, they dropped some of their costlier friends and concentrated on the true value of folks they came to enjoy all that much more.

Fortunately both had a good sense of humor about the exercise. They didn't mind saving a little more to increase their retirement-income potential. Theirs was a successful and not unpleasant exercise in getting everything ready so that retirement was sure to work out well for them.

Dress Rehearsals for Retirement

The daughter of an Eastern physician told us in detail about how her parents switched from seacoast luxury-hotel winter vacations and from luxury cruises to the far-out islands to a more modest mode of apartment dwelling in the same Southern climate they had come to appreciate and which they enjoyed with special friends. From former costly cruises they switched to new experiences by taking tramp-steamer trips.

I'm told they traded costlier strong-drink cocktailing, and the marbled steak syndrome of heavy eating, for the pleasant experience of sampling new wines and experimenting with a new variety of simpler meals without sacrificing the gourmet attitudes they had learned to appreciate. This successful medical man and his wife really prepared for their retirement earlier, and so much better.

Also people of modest means can find retirement happiness. We are close to one particular employee-benefit director at a mill employing 1,500 people. Every worker approaching retirement gets a personalized review about his pension and retirement situation prior to age 60, again prior to age 62, and eventually near age 65. The employee is encouraged to consider which choices will be most attractive to him and his wife. The wife is brought to one or more of these sessions. After each retirement this particular director keeps in close contact with each retiree. He invites them to bring their most harried problems to his attention in the hope that he might suggest where help might be found. Almost all of his "clients" retire on Social Security and a modest pension from the company, plus a little from a union retirement fund. The employees appreciate what they get because their expectations are quite realistic, and they depend on their pension director's helpful interest.

Save Yourself — Your Highest Asset

Don't forget when you're adding up assets to take special note of your health. You may feel weary and worn out before you step across the retirement threshold. But if you're still working you're still healthy enough for the time that's left through God's grace. Remember that health is still the first wealth.

Finally we are all worth more than we think. If you have paid in maximums to Social Security and if you are planning to retire at age 62, you and your wife have standing in the Social Security system an account at this moment, depending upon the average life expectancy for both of you, a sum beyond $50,000. May we repeat that? A sum exceeding $50,000 is ready at Social Security to be paid out to you as monthly income. That's a pretty good base to build on. True, you can't really live on Social Security alone. And yet we have witnessed people who are doing it, even in the sunny South. Most people also have some kind of pension from their career employment. Many have expected annuity income. Most have a little savings. Some have investments in real estate or in some modest stocks or bonds.

Most Are Worth More

We have no intention of indicating that the average human family is full of fat cats. Many are indeed quite poor. But in the middle of life in the middle of our society, people die and leave money to their survivors which they in their declining years did not know how to use and enjoy for a more creative retirement.

There are some things about money for retirement that need restating. Again and again!

You will probably have less income when you retire. This reality should not come as a surprise to any of us.

It is also possible to practice to live on less before you reach that moment of problem or opportunity.

It is increasingly evident that also people of modest means can find happiness. This depends on your attitude and how you have been rehearsing for this promised land.

What is also apparent is that you do not need to be poor in spirit even though your means may be modest. A recent medical magazine article asked, "Is there a life after work?" That depends. For an increasing number of enlightened retirees who have looked and planned ahead there is indeed a life after all that work is done.

If you are not yet certain how your retirement attitude will shape up, consider the alternatives. Lots of couples arrive at retirement with one partner already gone. Many are in limited health.

Factor Life's Remaining Income

We met a man in New England who was by his own admission only a modest success. In our view he was a giant of sorts. He and his wife had lived cautiously and always worried about their security. And yet they had saved some net worth.

When he retired at age 58 he paid himself a salary from existing assets and from what he might still earn from part-time jobs.

He factored his life expectancy to age 80 and figured that with Social Security, with the most modest of pensions, and with earnings his assets would produce, his life's savings would last until he was 80 plus years of age.

By switching assets into income-producing security, he gained the comfort of psychological security, and he and his wife went on with the task and pleasure of living the rest of their lives with faith and confidence.

You don't have to be "poor in spirit"—or quite as provident as our friend in New England—but money need not be your biggest problem in retirement.

Retirement Preparation Exercises

● Organize a retirement cost-of-living budget.
● Compare that to today's cost-of-living.
● How wide is the gap? How serious is it?
● What will your income be? From which sources?
● Note six ways to economize—without self-pity.

CHAPTER 3

Where to Live in Retirement

The first warning — at least a friendly caution — about where to live in retirement is: *Beware of Moving!*

Where to live is a little like some problems about money. Where can you afford to live? Where must you live for health reasons? Where should you live because of obligations and related circumstances?

Where do you want to live — both of you? And for what delightful and exciting reasons do you wish to live there?

One of my more expressive friends said this about the choice of where to live in retirement: whether to remain in the comfortable cocoon of familiar circumstance, or whether to flutter forth like the free butterfly to taste of new and unfamiliar blossoms in all the world's gardens.

Should You Stay — Or Might You Go

We heard a sensible dialog between two couples. One couple had deep roots and lots of warm family ties. They were determined to remain close to these because the wife was dependent on loving relationships with cousins, aunts, and uncles. Even friends were all tangled together in happy and familiar comfort.

The other couple were free spirits. They wanted to "make up for lost time," going where it was either warmer or cooler than where they had always lived, where there would be plenty of sandy beaches and sunny skies, and where recreation was more of a year-around thing. They didn't hold as fast to the old and familiar because they made friends easily, anywhere. They wanted to travel. It was fascinating to hear honest and good reasons on both sides of this "where to live in retirement" question. It passes through the minds of most of us.

Should we stay or dare we move? What kind of housing? Where? Can we afford to own, or would it be simpler and cheaper to rent and remain mobile?

Avoid Trading New Problems for Old

There are lots of mirages in this question. We've seen people exchange one set of problems they couldn't handle for another set they didn't even want to learn how to manage. Getting rid of a paid-for old house because "we don't need all that room" is one logical view. But often moving into inexpensive and cramped quarters in new and unfamiliar areas can introduce a new kind of loneliness. Actually it can grow out of "all that new togetherness."

The one principal premise that cannot be repeated too often or too strongly is that you "beware of moving" until you have gone there; until you have lived for a reasonably representative time (and vacations are not always representative); until you have made comparisons between the cost of one against the unfamiliar expense of the other. And in all of this sampling, it seems to work best if it's done over a period of time—*beforehand*—without upsetting or uprooting the shelters of the old, familiar homestead.

Many people retire and "pull up stakes" to move to a gentler climate. They do this to meet the needs of one of the retired partners or sometimes of both of them. But things happen—or don't happen—in the new place. They don't know anyone and don't find it easy to meet new people. Retirement relocation *loneliness* is a fact that can quickly destroy the joy of all this wonderful, new sunshine and sky.

Tough to Come Home — Unsuccessfully

Remember this caution: It's very difficult, like in Humpty-Dumpty, to put it all together again once you have upset the comfortable and familiar. And it isn't usually necessary. It's fun to look around, like the bee and the butterfly, to see what you can see, to sample different kinds of relaxed living, and to do it well in advance without commitment and without upsetting the security of your home base.

The certain point is that many people do relocate and do so happily. We have observed that those who do it best are the ones who have tried it out beforehand over a period of time. On the other hand, some people should stay behind and keep those home fires burning within familiar neighborhoods or within family-and-friend relationships. There may be a lot of things wrong with where you live, but you'll find all kinds of new things wrong in some of the places where you might move. Try it before you buy it!

Some people should move away for reasons of health, to provide more year-around exercise opportunity, or to create new interests and excitement that sometimes happen when we get outside of familiar ruts.

Climates Are Only Different

Take care to avoid thinking that climate is all that vital in retirement. Hundreds of thousands of people live in all of the extremes of climate variety and remain there. Some go away and miss contrasting extremes and pine to return. Climate is a personal matter for so many reasons. Personal preferences and physical well-being enter in.

Many have little free choice about whether to move or stay. We know many people who must conserve their energy and their resources by moving in with family. Are you willing to try it?

Are you smart enough to avoid "selling out everything" and giving it to the relative who will take you in? Too often that ends up being the most unsatisfactory. In spite of all past loving relationships, something can happen so that you will really "be taken in."

We have observed that careful planning protects on this problem. It protects all parties. We see another necessity, namely: Fight to retain control of your own circumstances. Stay independent from the decisions of others as long as you physically or financially can. Difficult as it may be, strive to stay in charge of your own problems and solutions.

Some Seek Balanced Societies

Upon leaving a southern church one Sunday this writer's wife spoke in response to an unstated question, "I've decided that I certainly don't want to live here in the midst of all those very old people. I prefer meeting people of all ages."

We told this to a friend who said that his grandson had gone to church with him on about the same Sunday in another senior-citizen mecca in another southern area. After church the grandson said, "Grandpa, where were all the people? Where were all the kids and the mommies and daddies?" He saw only "grandpas and grandmas." True, as they get older many can't manage the enthusiasm and excitement of the young. Others miss terribly the blending of all of society's families and miss the normal family and neighborhood interrelationships they grew up with.

Experts say that older people should try to stay as flexible and as integrated in society as their age and weather adaptabilities permit. Minds will wither if not challenged, "quicker than a cucumber on the vine."

There are no perfect answers for all aging. But there is necessity for those not yet retired, or soon approaching that time, to do some roaming about to check out new frontiers.

Costs Are Often Similar

A word about costs of living here or there. We see people of modest circumstances living right where they always lived or, in modest adjustments of these familiar circumstances, in a smaller home or a little apartment close to church, friends, and family. We also find these same kinds of people with little or nothing more than Social Security living in gentler climates, in small houses outside of expensive cities and away from costly beaches. We find them in mobile-home parks where a new kind of neighborhood with new friends offers a variety of living at modest monthly costs.

Lots of people in both the above-mentioned categories tell us they like to keep their living circumstances simple because they want to visit scattered families and friends— not just remain always in the same place.

Back to the dialog of the two couples who were at divergent views about whether to stay or to move away: They finally, half-seriously and half-kiddingly, promised each other that the free-spirit couple would move to new circumstances so that they could look about and sample all the beckoning world out there. The other was determined to remain "back home." Each admitted that they may sometimes wish to have a little of the other. And so they worked out a periodic exchanging of their living circumstances, so that those in their cocoon could flit about a little and the "butterflies" could settle back into familiar gardens for occasional renewing of old ties.

We thought it a wonderful "best of both worlds" answer, even if it seems impractical or whimsical to you now.

More might be made of such periodic exchanging of living circumstances. It could give us chances to vacation away without the burden of double maintenance costs.

Keep One Foot on Familiar Ground

Keep your "where to live" options open as long as you can.

Several sensible acquaintances are sampling the Southwest, the Southeast, and the Northeast, but they are holding onto their home base while they go through six months here, six months there. Many will say that's all right for the wealthy. But the people we are speaking of are *not* that rich except in flexibility and imagination. We have seen people of modest means work out the details of such experiments and make them work.

Where to live in retirement? We have found a very good way to work out perplexing problems like this: Make a list of unanswered questions. On a separate sheet list the obvious pros and cons of moving or staying—or, if need be, to move in with someone or into senior-citizen housing.

We are aware that some are already old, weary, and perhaps not well. Many of our blithe suggestions have little value in circumstances like these which will eventually come to most of us. But do make pro and con lists if you still have the option to decide. Set down your own most personal and joyful wishes. Remember that retirement is a free choice with lots of "*free* time" and with freedom for deciding on new ways to live for the rest of your lives. Gone are some of the restrictions which tied you to a specific place because of job and family obligations. You can live anywhere you like within your circumstances.

Consider your alternatives. Add still one more new dimension during your lifetime. There is no injustice in this to anyone. Be as nice as you can to yourselves.

Rehearse—And Return if You Like

Beware of one remaining trap! Don't wait too long to try new pastures. Go while you still have psychic energy and excitement enough to try. Make it a joyful effort, even if it means ultimately staying right at home. Decide and abide! But finally, make still one more arrangement.

Where Survivor Will Finally Be

Where shall the surviving partner wish to be when he or she reaches the fact of being left behind?

Would you rush "back home" or try to make a new life among new friends in new places? We see people doing it both ways—successfully *and* unsuccessfully. The question suggests you build in a few more options so that you will, as candidly as you are able, discuss this fuzzy detail in advance. I know many of you will say, "I don't like to think of those things." Who does? On the other hand, it's no real kindness to leave your partner in the grip of uncertainty, to force or permit rash or wrong decisions about where "I will stay when I'm all alone."

Look ahead; look around; look into all of your options and then, whether you move or stay, remember there's no place like a loving home, wherever it may finally be.

Retirement Preparation Exercises

- List the pros and cons of your housing needs.
- Check out comparative costs of owning and renting.
- Compare living costs "here" compared to "there."
- As a couple list reasons for staying; for moving.
- Give each other a note expressing your own survivor wishes.

CHAPTER 4

How Will You Keep Busy?

Retirement promises plenty of free time—lots of free time for the retired person—whether he knows what to do with it or not.

Time has been called the worst enemy or the best friend of retired persons. Well into his seventies now, a neighbor says he's so busy in retirement that he's thinking of "putting on another man." Another true cliche says it another way: "I don't know how I ever had time for my job, I'm so busy since I'm retired."

The trick is to avoid new routines of time-killing nothingness unless that's exactly what you want to do with all that free time.

But how about thinking of the free time of retirement as a gift—a gift of 15 to 30 years of "anything you want to do." Not everything, mind you! A selective something you simply must pursue, whether it be for love, fun, money, or for any combination of these.

It's Easier—With a "Boss"

It helps to have an agenda for being out of work. You don't have a boss telling you what to do anymore. You don't have job assignments, quotas to meet, piecework to get out on time, so many miles to travel, and so many sales to make.

Now you're unstructured or soon will be. You have no

agenda unless you make one. Why not dig back into all those overflowing drawers of dreams of postponed ideas which always carried the familiar alibi: "If I ever have enough time"?

Now you'll have enough time, but it will take a certain discipline to make that gift of time work for you.

Do a little research of your own. Go where senior citizens sit and watch the world go by with a remembering smile, or sit and stare vacantly, waiting for another day to pass.

Try Giving of Yourself: That's Living

Living in old age offers the retired person just that: Living! Your name comes off the door. Your phone may not be ringing much. There is little you have to do. That's enough to make any person feel unimportant and unneeded.

Fight it, friend! Fight it in the most cheerful and most exciting way you can. All these promises of exciting new things to do sometimes bring out a critical comment from practical hardheads. They say that it's okay to preach "do what you want to do" and "why not begin doing it?" But they suggest that not all people have the same kind of creative resources. Not all people know exactly what they'd like to do or know how to find out. That's·our job—to help them find ways. A few new ways!

Find New Worlds of Wonder

Take this older couple we've witnessed in their middle seventies, holding each other's hand as much in fear of falling as in love. They walked gingerly, haltingly over uneven fields near the simple cottage where they lived at the edge of a medium-sized town. They came to a building which was unfamiliar to them. They peered in its window to see what went on there. And some good soul inside stepped outside to invite them in. "This is a curative workshop for retarded children. Would you help us with this little boy? He can't manage by himself. Needs someone to feed him. This little girl likes the water. We are teaching her to swim. But she's afraid of falling and sinking. You see, she can't walk like you and I. Would you stay a while to help us? Just as persons — not teachers. The children will be so happy to have you."

But the old couple felt too old for this kind of activity and responsibility. They hadn't volunteered. They were simply drafted by a wise young person who saw their need as well as the children's. He saw that they might blend beautifully together. They didn't get paid — not in money. They were asked to come back next day, and the day after that, and on and on. They were admonished by the staff not to get sick and not to fail to show up because the little boy depended on "Grandma" to help him eat. He was handicapped and retarded. She helped and he smiled in return. The old "Grandpa" had found a new "granddaughter" in the little girl he helped to dinner, to therapy, and to the swimming pool. The pay they got was the importance of being needed as humans to love the unloved, to help the helpless.

This old couple had formerly worried about time — and their circumstance. Now they're worried lest they should fall or become ill and miss being at the workshop for the retarded. What a wonderful gift of life and love each gave the other! It cost nothing really — and it paid in being wanted and needed.

As People We Need Other Humans

You may not feel creative about what you want to do with yourself and your time. But you can be! A man we know became aware of blind people and wondered how they kept up on the day's news. He called one and offered to read the newspaper over the telephone each day. Now he enjoys the daily visit with five blind friends to whom he brings the day's current events. And he and they have new friends.

How About Self-Concerned Interests?

It's not necessary for everyone to pick up do-good activities if other self-concerned interests beckon. Why not explore retirement as the time of opportunity for a new career? For another career? For a part-time career? As an avocational activity for which there never was enough time or opportunity? For love or money—or just for the fun of it? There's nothing wrong with augmenting income with a little part-time work if that happens. Some protest, "If you suggest that I work after I'm retired, why should I retire?" The point we make is that you *are going* to be retired sometime. You'll be better off if you keep activity options going for you.

Try Library Reference—It's a Gold Mine

For some, dealing with groups of people has become tiring or bothersome. Find a one-to-one relationship. Seek out resources at your local libraries, at your church, area social organizations, or the various welfare offices in your town or county. Find unresolved problems to which you might relate for an opportunity to grow as a person. An organization in our area has a phone number people can call if they have trouble. One older "client" gentleman became a burdensome nuisance. He had found a friend to fill his loneliness at the other end of the emergency line. He kept calling and calling. Finally he had to be helped out of his new problem because he was "hogging" volunteer time, selfishly keeping them from serving others. Because he was in need of human contact, and such a

31

terribly boring talker in his zeal to hang on and communicate once he had found a friend, he was asked to do the same for others. He was given a few names of people to call—or people who would call him when they had trouble. Now these people help each other on a new one-to-one basis. His liability becomes their asset.

Second Careers—Better than the First

There are ways to solve the harnessing of time.

Suppose you really want to reach out and do a brand-new thing. Why not? Why not become a sculptor, a painter, a writer, a speaker? Who says you can't? Serve yourself, and your neighbor as well? There's so much that goes undone in the world because so many don't know where to begin. What are you good at? Are you a housewife with a grandmotherly interest in children's clothes? Are you a man who knows all about hunting and fishing equipment? Or cameras? Or small engines? Or plumbing? Retired folks we have seen who have opened themselves up to these small, personal-service kinds of odd jobs seem to have their hands full. There appears to be more work than they can handle. We find wives of some senior citizens who protect their too-busy husbands by announcing that "he's got too much to do" or "he can't take on one more job." Wise wife! Perhaps! But it does indicate that lots of things need doing—*your* doing!

Wherever You Live—Others Also Live

If you move to a new area, there are lots of service jobs and discount-store sales opportunities which many can do. You can use your knowledge and expertise in things like sewing, fixing, taking pictures, or going fishing.

Sell paint and give painting advice from the knowledge of having painted around your own house; from fixing know-how you picked up.

The world and you and I need each other, but we may have to hunt around so that we find each other.

Moderation — Variation — Salvation

There are some things you should do about keeping busy. You have to stay well. Watch your eating and get enough rest. And exercise, not as medicine but for vitality and for feeling alive!

Try the joy of walking if you want to "see" the world you are living in. We sit around and ponder how to exercise. Walk! Swim! Bicycle! Or play games appropriate to your age and condition.

Part of the joy of extra time is the chance for social games with friends. Games are catalysts for deepening friendships — now that we all have more time. Make it happen.

Have you thought of becoming a student again? Isn't there something you always wanted to know about in detail and depth? Study — and become expert in anything that interests you. Get excited; become an expert and watch your ego grow!

Ever Looked into His Vineyard?

There's always been this postponed hope about doing a better job of serving the Lord by serving your neighbor. Your neighbor still needs you. And the Lord needs your help. Ask Him for a list — for neighbors who need *you!*

The world needs your talent, even though you may think it too little. If it is much, you owe it all the more. Retirement is a gift of free time. This free time — and your talent to use it for yourself *and* for others — is still accountable.

Afraid of being bored and lonely? You can decide not to be lonely. How? By helping some other lonely person overcome his aloneness. Both of you gain.

We know of two older ladies who call each other every day at five o'clock to have a social drink together — over the telephone. It's cocktail communications, whether it be coffee, tea, or something more vibrant. They don't want to be alone each day. They don't want to drink alone; so they relate by telephone because that's what's available. Each day they bring a little love and pleasant chatter to each other. And the best part is that each has this wonderful extra gift of anticipating the next visit. Keep pleasant and expected contacts alive.

Loneliness is most often a decision you can make — to suffer or to overcome. If you're bored, reach out and find someone like yourself, or one *even poorer* in spirit. Find out what he or she needs from you.

We fret about the young. We worry about the old. Each group has its own wisdom to share. You may not be a teacher or a preacher but you can serve others. Tutor beginning piano or painting students. Bring homemade soup to the sick. Visit the shut-ins. Write letters for your arthritic friends before arthritis joins your joints.

What self-concerns have you to share — with neighbors you haven't even met? What will keep you happily busy?

Retirement Preparation Exercises:

- List part-time job ideas, opportunities.
- Chart three vital things you might like to try to do.
- Investigate courses to equip you for a "new thing."
- Any two interests — or activities — you can both share?
- List five types — groups — of people who may need you.

CHAPTER 5

It Helps to Stay Healthy

Health is such a personal thing. Our state of well-being is based on so many factors which are not always under our control. Perhaps they ought to be. But we are, after all, human and not as competent about managing ourselves as we like to think we are about managing for others.

If health is still the first wealth (and who can feel really rich if his health fails seriously?) there are a few basic facts which bear repeating.

Save Yourself — for Retirement

The single most important thing you must save for retirement is your health — or as much of it as you can hang onto as long and as happily as you can.

Health is subjective and is often based on such a personal point of view as how our attitude happens to be that particular day. As we grow older we notice that almost everybody has some aches and pains. Some just celebrate them more. This is not to say that it's wise to deny our physical limitations or hide from signs of little illnesses which can grow into big ones.

We all hear this cheery greeting: "How are you?" It's a greeting! It means "Hello" and "Nice to see you." We believe the greeter wants to know how we feel, so we begin to detail our attitude, our aches and pains — minutely and

35

thoroughly. A far better answer, if we are strong enough to manage such philosophy, is: *"I feel fine!"* The more you say it, the more it will be true.

We are not suggesting that specific ailments or real physical and emotional traumas will disappear just because we claim to feel fine. But they will go away—away, to the backs of our awareness.

Something to Get Up for—Every Day

There's so much real power in how you view things, how you think about life and your condition. It has been said that your attitude can kill you! We see this often in reluctant retirees who feel they no longer have any role to play; no former importance to feel buoyed up about; no place to go with high purpose; less money to do everything with. This phenomenon has been called the "age-66 syndrome"—a time and circumstance over which many men and their wives happily hop, onto long and continually active lives. But many unprepared men give up, and since they have nothing left to live for, they die.

It's not always an attitude ailment, of course. Experts on aging have studied the problem scientifically. They insist that a fierce desire to stay involved—to hang on to life—has actually prolonged the living years for many people whose days really had seemed numbered due to conditions they accepted or overcame.

Not very many of us can prolong our lives unnaturally. Nor can we change the state of our health substantially. But it is surprising to witness how much an early and interested attention to nutrition and exercise can add to our life span—how much extra time it adds to that we are blessed with as Providence smiles on us.

What We Don't Eat Can't Hurt Us

Much has been made of balanced diets, and a little more

should be said for *not* eating too richly in retirement. Think of all that extra time for all those fatty and fancy delights we love to revel in! The best case can be made for simplicity in what we eat; not how much of it we try to stoke away. The same goes for walking or biking instead of always piling into the family wagon—even for picking up a loaf of bread when the store may be just a good hike away.

Exercise is necessary to keep you vibrantly alive—to keep you alive longer; to keep your circulation circulating.

Another word of unworried caution: It is enlightened self-concern as you get older to develop better personal safety. Be aware of the risk of falling; of the mounting frequency of traffic dangers. If you drive, do so defensively by anticipating other drivers.

It is such a sad waste of time for living—of money and convenience—to become painfully and expensively laid up as the result of an avoidable accident.

Move more calmly with eyes wide open and in focus—and your attention turned on.

In retired lives, moderation is a special virtue. Moderation addresses itself to those excesses some of us indulge in, like smoking too much, drinking too much, sleeping too little, or, surprisingly, sleeping too much.

Doctors increasingly question their patients about when they eat the main meal each retired day. If in the evening, do you sit around with the undigested burden on your TV-watching mind? Trundling off to bed for lengthy hibernation? Sleeping too long without working off any of it in walking or moderate exercise? Excesses apparently exact their price in lessened lung and liver life and in stepped-up circulatory deterioration.

We are simply echoing doctors' sincere concern for your life, for a longer, vital span of life.

One of our most admired aging ladies (she never seems to be the grandmother she surely and proudly is) has a surefire recipe for facing the sometimes not-so-golden years. At her bedside she has this prayerful and humble reminder: "I'm not getting older – I'm just living longer." Find your own motto or proverb; or create one, like: "Lord, I thank You for each blessed extra day."

Remember Busy Grandma!

It's clear that remaining calm, cool, and "connected" is worth extra years for most of us. Many a busy grandmother used to be too busy to be sick, too needed to die. She stayed necessarily busy, always involved, always understanding the bigger needs of the rest of us. Who worried much over her aches and pains? They were often apparent. But there was so little time for Grandma to "enjoy" them. They either passed or fell into a blessed perspective. She was needed! She didn't dare quit – especially quit living! And so she lived – for others!

It's sensible for us to expect and accept some illness and some deterioration as we grow older. Let's look around and see how many of our friends have already stepped off of life's busy bus. How few of us will viably reach the four-score bonus-time of life! Vitamins may keep us going longer and antibiotics and other miraculous potions keep us alive longer, but that's not the "living" we're talking about. For those who can manage any choice, I beseech you to stay fiercely involved. Remain *important* to somebody! Important to yourself as well!

Accept Love – Give Love – It Warms

Sensitivity and concern are a two-way street. Accept the compassion of others for your own well-being and repay such concerns with warm empathy toward them.

Remember to thank your God for the years you have had in which to do His work and *your own*. Accept your afflictions and grow with them in order to accomplish more of your life's assignment.

There are all kinds of illnesses which sap the living from our tissues. There are some burdens that hurt more than broken bones. It's no secret that we are in a time of great awareness. Perhaps it's a time of being able to afford more self-searching. We are living amidst emotional conditions of many kinds.

"Nerves" and apprehensions are not necessarily imagined. Many people are confined to hospitals or suffer physical and mental distresses. Something they can't manage is keeping them from being well. It doesn't help the patient to hear again that "sickness" is psychosomatic or psychological. He is still sick!

Joy and Love Pay Off in Peace

If we could remain better students of life perhaps we could learn to anticipate and respond to the reasonable certainty that we will experience stresses we may find difficult to cope with. Mental health experts teach that it isn't the stress that's killing us but how we respond to the stresses we encounter.

Some may reach the "point of no return" when it comes to stress. But if we hold fast to a strong faith and trust in God's providence and in His helpful, watchful guidance of our lives, we need not fight all of our personal wars by ourselves. Calm trust in the love and help of neighbors and in our Maker can help keep us healthier longer. Finally for our benefit there are pills and potions and therapeutic medical practices which do help stabilize *and* tranquilize.

Let us accept our physical and mental energy and be grateful for it. Let us bless the Lord for our happy rewards and also for our troubled burdens. These can make us strong if we permit them to be strengthening. We do what

39

we can. We go for help humbly when it is clearly necessary. It is seldom wise to hide from the burdens of our times, to deny our inability to handle our assorted problems. Today we more honestly accept our limitations. That must be the beginning of a new degree of well-being for us.

Self-Esteem—Positive Personal Power

There must be great physical and psychological power in the knowledge of our true self-worth. If we are constantly concerned with distorted and diminishing self-esteem, we are adding destructive damage to our psyches. If worry is our principal hobby, we will not be worth much to anyone—including ourselves.

It is not pollyannaish to dwell a bit more on what we *can do*—and at the same time to accept what we believe we can't do. These are realities! Some of us can roller skate and others have difficulty walking gracefully. Some can paint, sing, or entertain. Some of us feel quite dull. We become pretty much what we think we are. What's wrong, then, with thinking better of ourselves so that we may enjoy being "better"? This isn't make-believe. It isn't a violation of custom or code of law to expect oneself to become better, to add small cubits to our limited self-stature. Try it, and as they say in modern merchandising, "you'll *like* it."

We Are Part of a Cycle of Living

There's a reality about being older. You tire more quickly. You have less resistance and are less able to maintain prolonged outputs of energy. Accept the fact that there's a little less of you—less than you thought when you were twenty. There is less on almost all counts—except in available self-esteem. Save yourself—for living! Don't keep squandering your psychic and physical energies on foolish and pointless problems. There are larger tasks on your assignment agenda. Live to be active and helpful.

Encourage and lead others out of *their* boring, empty loneliness—out of *their* shut-in reality.

Finally we may as well stop hiding from death: from our own death and from the inevitable death of our loved ones. We must learn to accept death when its time comes. We need not throw away instinctive self-preservation. But we can accept as part of God's plan our own death in the time of His choice and when our share of His work is done.

It's the Christian way to bring faith to bear on death and bereavement. As those entrusting the issues of life and death to God, who in His Son Jesus Christ loves us, we can help others—help them face their fear about imminent death. This is better in the long run than to keep saying that everything or everyone is going to be "all right." When the time comes for terminal patients, they are usually aware of it, but many are afraid and lonely. So few know how to help them face their own understanding of their real condition. So few of us can compassionately share in and help their troubled concerns. Before we can be of help, we need to face the facts ourselves, including the fact that "our Savior Christ Jesus . . . abolished death and brought life and immortality to light through the Gospel." (2 Timothy 1:10)

Be Needed—And Stay Strong

It helps if we stay healthy so that we can keep on living and serving. It must also be expected of us that we learn to accept the fact of our changing conditions. It must finally be self-evident in our older years that the curtain is beginning to come down. How well will you respond?

To avoid preoccupation with your physical condition, have annual check-ups—oftener if indicated—and abide by the advice of your doctor. Keep tab on the seven signals of cancer and on evident circulation disorders. Keep a mouth as full as possible of teeth and as empty as possible of the wrong kinds of food. Get plenty of fresh air and exercise. And, most important, try to maintain healthy and happy attitudes.

Retirement Preparation Exercises

- Work out simple eating, drinking, resting, and exercising regimens. Make these a routine for daily living.
- List three people who need you the way you are.
- Record — and communicate — any special health care you must receive.
- Dwell on the health concerns of those about you — rather than on your own.
- Investigate any decisions you can make about your own departure from life.

CHAPTER 6

Retirement and Aging: Keep It Legal

So many changes keep happening to us as we march toward our own aging and retirement. It seems that it ought to be more simple. But there are so many practical requirements we must face as our circumstances change and as the possibility increases that one of us may no longer be around.

Everyone asks it, and yet too few do anything about the question: Do you have a will? Do you *both* have a will? Do you know that you just about have to have a will these days in order to make your death 'possible'? Let's put it another way: If you don't have a will, things are going to be pretty impossible for those who remain after you have shuffled off.

Why must that be? Legal affairs with regard to retirement, and as they relate to the aging, are concerned with the rights of society and the rights of the people involved. Included are your rights, to be sure, but also the rights of those who are officially part of your family. It is up to you to designate the provisions of your will specifically and formally in writing, as well as the terms that have been altered by you in later codicils.

The Law Protects—You and Society

Wills record what your wishes are. They make your

decisions official. It isn't necessarily automatic that your wife will "get it all," or that she'll even get half of what's left. That is not automatically so and not for certain. It will not be our purpose here to wear the mantle of an attorney or a probate judge. Those are the people you ought to get to know before they get to know your survivors — too often unhappily.

We're coming face to face with very real facts when we look ahead toward that time when our so-called rights will have ceased with the end of our life and the rights of other people will have taken over. We ought to be sure that these "other people" include the ones we want and exclude the ones we don't want to have listed as official survivors to share in the inheritance of our property's remainder.

That's what legal affairs are principally about with regard to preretirement planning.

Think of It as Legal Housekeeping

There's such a simple view that can be put on these legal affairs which relate to retirement planning. We should simply be tidying up the actual and mental details of our specific property and personal possessions so that we can go into retirement with an unburdened mind — so that we can know in our heart that things are "arranged for" if, as they say, "the unforeseen should happen."

The unforeseen does happen to all of us as individuals and as families. And nowadays too often the unforeseen can include what is called a common disaster and, believe me, that opens up a whole new set of lawbooks.

I know that all this legal fussing must sound pretentious for a lot of us who were just modestly successful, who led simple lives with uncomplicated property and investments to worry about. We think we don't have anything to fuss about — no estate and precious little to leave for those who remain behind.

44

Well, this may come as a surprise to you. You should realize that the tax authorities of federal and state jurisdictions are very keenly interested in your "estate" and in the fact of your death when it happens. They move right up to the front of the line with their open basket. They are determined and certain to get their fair share. Usually they get theirs first, even if there is not enough property in liquid form to pay what is due to the taxing jurisdictions. They find it before anyone else may have it. You may wonder where it will come from.

Yes, wills do make dying "possible." But wills also express your (both of your) specific wishes and plans.

Remember, the law protects you *and* society. And the laws ordained for society may not always be exactly in accord with your own personal wishes. That's because the laws and the courts cannot know what is in your heart, what the nature of your family relationships are, and how you view these.

Unrecorded Wishes — Not Official or Automatic

You have the opportunity to personally decide about your property, according to your collaborative wishes as a partner in a marriage, or as a single or a remaining partner of a family. First, you must be provided for legally, for the use of whatever has been acquired and whatever property you still possess while you are living and dependent upon it. You think that's automatic? Oh, no! Believe me, these things can get complicated.

The principal thing you want to avoid is having you become dependent on someone else — either for your keep or for your decisions. You must face the fact that your aging life will bear down upon you, and some of you may lose part of your capability to make the best and most reasoned judgments. It may not be pleasant to contemplate. For one reason or another you may lose part of your competence—not necessarily in your opinion but in the opinion of the courts and other members of your dependent family. Some of those "family members" may not be *dependent* upon you, but they *may be* depending on you to leave them "a bundle," however large or small that may be. Remember, the law protects society, and they are part of that society.

Seek Preventive Legal Guidance

Look for the most trusted legal advice you can find in your area. Depend on the experienced suggestions of trusted friends who know which attorney would understand and would be most concerned about your affairs.

If you neglect to take this action now because you think there's lots of time, you place your survivors in a position where your inaction can actually punish them or short-change and cheat them out of their just due—out of what you would have wished for them to inherit. None of us lives forever, and even that "forever" keeps being interrupted in unexpected ways in more and more families.

Neglect and delay do leave a terrible mess. You should go down to the courthouse and sit in on the settlement of estate matters or attend trials that result from this kind of neglect. You would quickly see with some alarm what you must do right now before that "unforeseen" thing happens.

Even the Poor Possess Estates

Oh, I know, you'll say: "We've always been poor and have so little to fight over; we surely have no so-called 'legal affairs.'" Wrong again! That's where the law that protects society comes in. It protects the rights of the poor, the rich, and the in-between. Yes, you surely do have legal affairs that need attention beforehand.

You don't have to glorify your impoverished condition, if that's your reality, but wouldn't you like to make sure that it's fair? Fair to your surviving partner? And wouldn't you like to avoid excessive and unnecessary taxation of the remainder of your property upon your death? There are steps you can take now. You'll need financial and legal advice to get it all in order. Our role is simply to arouse your concern so that you will take action.

It's a new ball game after you die. There are new players, and new rules go into effect. You won't be around to officiate in your familiar role as family umpire anymore. So you have to state what you have in mind for each specific member of your family, for your wife, for your church or other organizations in which you have a continuing and supporting interest. How do you want your husband or wife to manage until his or her death?—until the remainder of your property gets redistributed? Will you want your assets to pass directly over to your surviving children and grandchildren? To which ones? To which ones not? You had better do some homework if your retirement is going to be very rewarding and if the memory of "good old Mom and Dad" is going to be much of a happy memory.

Promises in Writing Are Legal

So many families have such good relationships with each other and with their children that it's a beauty to behold. As they go through life they casually promise each other this heirloom or that. A daughter admires some crystal. A son would like one day to own Dad's wonderful set of tools or a watch, or Grandpa's war mementos. And they are sincerely promised by loving parents who are still living.

And then one day Mom and Dad aren't there anymore. And the children (worse yet, neighbors or grasping strangers) come in to "take care of some of these nicer things" before they get all tied up in the hands of attorneys

47

and such. You know what? Sally is not apt to get your crystal, Mom, unless you write it down officially and have it recorded. It is also wise to share such written information with Sally—or with Bobby, Tommy, Nellie, and the rest.

Promises you have made and wishes you might have expressed should be officially written, recorded, and shared with the expected recipient so that no one else can take these heirloom pieces for his own. If you want to make a gift, make it legally, firmly recorded officially.

The very best attorney, like the best doctor, keeps his client well. He is expert at preventive legal supervision to *keep* his clients out of trouble, not just to *get* them out of trouble. It costs much less to keep things legally well-ordered so that nothing can go wrong. Try preventive legal planning. I vigorously caution you to take steps *now:* with wills (both of you), trust agreements, and bequests you wish to have delivered after your death. Do this so that treasured mementos get into the right hands.

Each of us knows our family members, and we know our wishes. But the judge won't know those wishes. And the courts must protect the rights of all of society. So you have to indicate officially *what you want done* or *what must be done* when you are no longer present to manage for yourself.

Face Death—
As a Legal and Certain Reality

All of this "after we're gone" talk upsets some people. It especially upsets some wives because they do not like to think of the time when one of them will be missing. People hide foolishly from the realities of death, and that's one of the reasons it is often such a shock to so many of us. We hide from death, and since we are not very well acquainted with its realities beforehand, it comes as such a terrible surprise. Then we are filled with grief and too often with confused judgment.

I like the story about the deceased man whose will was opened and read by the attorney to the assembled family. They sat around expectantly to see what good old Dad had left for each. And the lawyer read: "Being of sound mind, I spent it all." Not provident perhaps, but amusing! This is some of the spirit we would like to will to you right now.

Why not tidy up your affairs? Do those legal things which official advisers keep harping about. Have things arranged to protect your family's rights and those of society —but according to your wishes. Then after you have made reasonable arrangements and have it all recorded officially, make further note to have it checked periodically and to bring things up to date from time to time. It's true: Our family and fiscal circumstances, and the facts of changing relationships in modern families, require periodic checking. We ought to make sure that when we arrive at the doorstep of our promised land, everything's going to be okay.

When you've done all this (and when you've collaborated with your partner) then plan for the living that's ahead of you—for the life you must still live.

Plan to go out and enjoy life. Live that life and relax about the end of it. You can't predict when that will be, and it's good that you cannot. Accept the fact that here's an area you're not in charge of. Accept the inevitability of the end of your life, but fight fiercely to live the rest of your life as joyfully as you can.

Use and Conserve Your "Rewards"

Do all you can psychologically and practically to see that you are really going to be entitled to keep and to enjoy your retirement reward. Conserve your health and your

49

sanity. Nurture your happiness as a person, as a member of your own segment of human society, as a family — a family of loving relatives and a family in the community of God. It is proper for you to have what you have labored for and what you have been prudent enough to save. Do all you can to keep it, so that now it may serve you as you have served for so long. View this time and your "physical property" as something to be used for good and as part of your reward for having worked hard and lived long. Thank God for that life! But don't make it a hollow victory by "carping" about how small your reward is — compared to what you'd always dreamed.

Be Slow to Sign — Seek Legal Advice

Don't take foolish risks now about signing things over to anyone without a great deal of legal caution. Use all the careful counsel you can bring to bear on your problem. Keep as much independence as you will need, so that you can make your own decisions as long as you are competent. Check with each other and decide what you want to do, where you want to live, how you want to enjoy your assets: your money, property, and yourselves. Decide how much you will want to share with those who have a greater need, with your church and its organizations. Serve the Lord and serve yourselves. This is just!

Enjoy the Fruits of Your Efforts

Financial people who are very conservative have been telling us that more and more people should begin carefully to inherit some of their own money, to enjoy some of their own assets. We all know the Puritan doctrine: "Never invade principal!" That's a philosophy — for the olden days. Don't cheat yourselves of your reward. Enjoy and share. Become a legally well-organized member of the family of God.

50

Retirement Preparation Exercises

- Arrange (both of you) for up-to-date wills. Do it now.
- Develop a trusted relationship with an attorney.
- Get tax-saving advice about death and estate taxes.
- If you made family promises, put them in writing and record them.
- Officially record your property in one name, *or* in both names, *or* in common—as advised.

CHAPTER 7

In Sickness, in Health—
Or in Dying

Into each life a little rain must fall, but sometimes it's more of a deluge. Not all of us will always be totally well. Some will be very sick; some for a long, long time.

Retirement and the years just before happen to come at a time of life when we are no longer kids. We are involved in the process of using ourselves up. We have worked and worried and scrimped and saved—and also enjoyed a good life. We're still alive, still kicking! And yet many of us keep complaining about how ailing we are or how poorly we feel. There seems to be something about the human spirit that requires it to wear this sackcloth of self-depreciation. Are we trying to make ourselves sound small when actually we think ourselves really quite big? Is this false humility with a hook?

Consider the Alternatives

Our body tissues get tired and our organs begin to fail from years of wear and tear, and all this is the natural end result of the aging process. If we are overconcerned with either the fact or our hobby of "enjoying poor health," or if we fear the thoughts of dying, we should be reminded of the alternatives. Some lifetime friends and family members are no longer with us. Death came and called more than we care to remember. But *we* are still hanging around!

The alternatives to feeling "down in the dumps" or being really ill are not very comforting but worth considering.

We may as well accept this certain reality: Death is an expected visitor, but we don't want that visit just yet.

Still Alive—And Really Living

How about trying to stay as alive as you can for as long as you can? Then you can do for others many of the things you probably did poorly for yourself. Think of all the shut-ins and the lonely who would be comforted by an occasional visit from you. There must be poetic justice in putting some kindnesses into the bank of human consideration so that you may hope to be remembered too. There is so much that needs doing. If you aren't creative enough to make your own list, we can give you one. Start right where you are—right in your own "acre of diamonds." Dig around and count the wasted talents, the time and resources you failed to share adequately. There is still time for better sharing.

Give Some of Yourself—To Others

Perhaps we only litter a little, but all thoughtless dropping by the way adds to the problem of pollution and to human injustice. What about the unfairness of isolation for our lesser brothers? Lesser to whom? Do we acquiesce in silence or actually contribute to their hopeless lives? Do we ever reach out and touch the unfortunate? What better time is there for that than right now as we approach the bonus years of our retirement? It is time to dedicate and recommit ourselves to love a neighbor we so often forget. We won't have to reach far to grasp the chance to lift somebody up. It's easier and more fun than holding him down.

We can all begin right where we are—with our own family and friends.

Love is a duty we owe our loved ones to help them live better, more fulfilling lives. But how exactly can we help? Encouragement is such a wonderful gift! It's easy to pass around. A few words of good cheer help people to help themselves; help them to *believe* in themselves. Remember when cheerful encouragement helped you?

Keep on the Good Side of Death

There is much being made today of the Christian duty to face the reality of dying, to actually play fair with terminally ill friends and relatives, to help them prepare to die.

We prefer to say to the very ill, "You look just great. You'll be out of here in no time." We say that, and it helps *us*—we don't feel as sad or guilty.

Those who study the phenomenon of death are convinced that most terminal patients are quite aware of their condition and fearfully sure they will soon die.

When Grandma Moses was asked about her eventual death, she said: "I think about death each day and expect its visit. Each day I awaken I know I have one more opportunity. When I retire and go to sleep, I never know when that happens or if I will awaken. Some day I will not awaken, but I won't know that I will have died, unaware of when death came. I am ready and not troubled about dying."

But the dying are lonely. They are treated thoughtlessly by most of us as we try to shelter them from the truth. Many patients have said it. They just want to talk a little reality with some loving person who will listen to their fears. They expect they are going to die and feel it's going to be all right. Most don't want to be shut up and turned off by phoney platitudes.

True, some patients probably should not be alarmed

54

into unnecessary and agonizing fears, especially if something of their condition still permits hope. But doctors know. Many nurses and visiting clergy understand. They know that the very ill patient needs someone to confide in, someone to listen to problems that concern him. Sometimes he has affairs he may want looked after when he's gone.

Help Others to Die with Dignity

Indeed, it is gaining favor to accept—and to stop denying—the reality of our own end and the reality of the deaths of loved ones.

We feel anger and suffer guilt feelings about grief. We haven't always measured up considerately or thoughtfully, or compassionately and lovingly. We *are* human. We needn't be ashamed of these guilt and anger reactions which may be part of our grief. But we are also grown and mature people who must face realities. We can't hide from death. Death arrives. It takes from us—or takes us.

Why not take a few practical steps with regard to death and bereavement for those you love and those who depend upon you? Why not plan and discuss who will take charge when the time comes? Make a few thoughtful arrangements now. It ought to be a good exercise because it turns a light on the dreaded darkness of death. The light of reality and understanding should focus on the certain fact that we won't always be together. What will the other partner do? How will we respond? Talk about it a little in fairness to the one who will remain behind. It's sound practice—a small preparation for that moment of our "retirement from life."

The Ultimate Selflessness

What steps can you agree on now? Do you want to give bodies or organs to science or medical schools? Does someone else need part of you—to keep going longer so that he may live out his unfinished life after yours is ended? Where do you stand on that question? Not all can do it. We recently attended a memorial service for one who gave his body to science. The compassionate clergyman spoke the simple and sensible prayer to God in behalf of the departed: "This is my body, which I now give up for You."

A realistic way to get started on the question of facing death beforehand, or facing such realities and problems which may soon face the other partner, is to express your own concerns and preferences and to share these in casual and candid discussion with your partner. Or do this with a close friend or relative in whom you can confide. By expressing your own wishes you raise similar points of view in the other person. You create understandings of where you both stand.

There doesn't seem to be much realism in hiding from death. The unexpected shock leaves too many details to chance—leaves too many scars which take too long to heal. It may not be a sensitive analogy, but we know that our aging auto will one day break down and cease to run. We will also run down, break down, and fall apart. Ultimately we too will cease to operate.

Some Promises Are Impossible to Keep

While we're looking ahead and making plans, it might be well to raise a caution about avoiding unrealistic promises and the risk of changed minds. Such unworkable commitments often stand in violation of the memory of the departed anyway. It's a kind of Christian compassion, perhaps, to heed the wishes of the other. But we have no right to tie the hands of eternity and to lock another person into emotional promises which were poorly made in a darkening time and sometimes for wrong reasons. Heed such wishes as you can, but heed as well the risky making of foolish promises.

When the moment arrives and you need to sacrifice some loved one who must return to his Maker, don't hang on and prolong the torment for all concerned. Let him go! We only have the loan of each other, as gifts. We do not possess. It is His wish when He calls one of us. With a graceful acceptance of the rightness of life, accept death when it comes.

Life must end—also for you and me. Live your life fully and as meaningfully as you can. Do for others! And do for your God, too! Live according to His wishes for you. And when your moment arrives, go in peace to your Father. Be satisfied that He wishes you to be there—with Him.

Retirement Preparation Exercises

- List five living goals you still hope to accomplish.
- Assist others to remain involved in living.
- Accept the certain fact of death—yours and theirs.
- Arrange officially for bequests of your body or individual organs (eyes, e.g.) if it is your desire to leave them for medical science.
- List, together if possible, each other's wishes. Determine who is to look after them afterward.

CHAPTER 8

How's Your Spiritual Health?

How does an ordinary layman counsel with his brothers and sisters about how to be at peace with God? How does one mature human say, in understandable ways to another, how to love and listen to Him?

Are you at peace with your God? Can you say with St. Paul (Romans 5:1), "Since we are justified by faith [faith in the redeeming, sin- and death-destroying merits of the Savior], we have peace with God through our Lord Jesus Christ"? If you have come to know God as your Father who loves and forgives you for the sake of Jesus Christ, you will feel comfortable with God. At peace with Him, you will be at peace with yourself; you will have a self-worthy feeling, an honest self-appreciation for yourself as a person in the human scheme of God's great earth. And you will be at peace with others, capable of listening to the joys and sorrowful cries of your neighbors and of loved ones close to you.

Find Some Good in "Anyone" — An Exercise

It's not always easy to like everyone. It isn't even re-quired·to like everything about everyone because so much is really not very likeable nor worthy of liking. Many of the neighbors whom we are expected to love are not very lovable. But can't we cease judging them so harshly? We can start by looking into their eyes and seeing into their hearts. This is not mystical nonsense.

We ourselves have found it a disquieting exercise sometimes to pause in our self-concern—and to interrupt our distaste for one of those unlovable neighbors—in order to listen to his needs, to hear him out, to sense his sensitivities, to feel perhaps even for just a moment some compassion for his troubled condition, to hear just once the real needs of another and to hear it louder than our own needs of that moment, to give of ourselves without holding back—even to someone not all that lovable.

Jesus didn't say all our neighbors would be attractive and charming. No one else promised it either.

Heartfelt Concern Will Create a Response

How do we develop heartfelt concern for those whom Christ puts in our way? Are we really Christian enough, and man and woman enough, to be worthy to be Christ's brother and to serve His brethren? By nature man is a sinner and is not worthy of any high honor or assignment. However, Christ died for us when we were yet unworthy sinners. He clothed us in the robes of righteousness *and* in the attire of a servant. He said we were now worthy not only to be kings and priests with Him but also to be His servants.

Too often we resent and criticize. We hold ourselves apart from those we fear or reject. Being a brother to our neighbor is the ultimate compliment, whether this brotherhood be within our family, within our circle of acquaintances, or within the larger human family.

Praying Is Like Any Other Exercise

True, we can't do all this spiritual health and maintenance work by ourselves. It's arrogant to think so. The Lord taught us to pray and we remember to lean on Him when we're in deep trouble.

How alive is our prayer life? Is it like so much of the

rest of our living? Not very alive, not very vigorous? Does our faith in the providence of our Master put our pleading in the prayerful perspective of a belief and trust in Him?

We've known some good and prayerful people of all ages. One we like to tell of was a simple man who sat in the last pew of his large church. He seemed only to look — never to rail at God or to pray piously. He came often, sitting smilingly and looking at his Lord. His pastor, seeking an insight into this simple man's praying, asked him to tell how he found such grace, such a prayer life. Our friend said, "Oh, it's quite simple; I just come to visit. I sit and look at Jesus, and He looks at me." Quite a prayer! No begging, just being!

Is it possible for us to know ourselves well enough to know how holy is our spirit? This is work for learned clergymen. But must it be only their business? There are many good men and women of all ages and in all conditions who live admirable lives of sharing, lives which are selfless and full of the Holy Spirit. At any event, it's probably not important for us to know how holy is our condition. It is enough for Him to know, and for us to follow His leading.

Love Is a Decision — An Attitude

But we can tell whether love lives in us. We can tell, and we do know how we relate to those who rely on us for support and encouragement, for the supporting hand of love which keeps them going and trying. We know if love lives in us because it is something to see reflected in our eyes. And we feel it in our hearts. It's part of our spiritual health.

We need not wear love on our sleeves and probably ought not anyway. But it is right to share our heart with those around us — and to do so with a little more than a smile. "Here, let me help you." "What can I do to lighten your load?" Too pietistic? I don't think so. It is especially appreciated by those of us who are getting a little older. It's just a small sample of the Golden Rule of life. It's that yardstick we require of others—toward ourselves.

Do you remember Christ and why He died and rose again? St. Paul teaches that He "was put to death for our trespasses and raised for our justification" (Romans 4:25), that is, to make us right with God. Christ died that we might come to life, both now (in that we live in Him and serve Him) and on the Last Day when He will return for our bodily resurrection. Is He also *your* Savior? Sometimes we fail to remember that it was we He had in mind all the while—you and I.

Beware of Becoming Too Comfortable

There is so much that's wrong—or seems to be. There is so much injustice, so much imbalance in the world's privileges and problems. They seem to be so unevenly distributed. We especially consider that distribution to be uneven and unfair if we don't always get our share of the good. Do we want to be too comfortable compared to our brothers and neighbors? Do we really deserve God's guiding friendship?

We ought to feel good in our faith. We ought to be joyful and loving. And trusting! If we rely on the providence of the Father, our faith ought to make us feel good. We are in His hands. The gift of ourselves—to share with others and to give back to God—must be the greatest gift we'll ever give.

If you think your spiritual health needs treatment, you're not hopeless. You're normal and alive! Alert to your reality! Sometimes we get all messed up and dreamy-eyed about the state of our well-being. When we are tempted to despair, even for a moment, we ought to re-

61

member: "Where else are our troubles always welcome?" Where else, indeed, but with God?

Happily Meditating Is Praying Too

If we are friends of Christ's and if we are His brothers and sisters, we know that our problems will get attention. But sometimes it seems that we forget. It is usually when our troubles get too "hot to handle" that most of us remember. That's when our prayer life really comes alive.

Must we always be cajoling, pleading, and railing at God to look after us? To make us better off than we are? Isn't it more realistic for struggling Christians to expect their religion—their faith—to become more of a relaxed relationship in which there is both speaking to God and listening to Him?

There are varied ways to listen to our Maker. Needless noises and distractions often intercept His messages. Give Him a private audience occasionally—not just for one-way conversations but also for listening to His answers.

If we believe that Scripture brings us truth, then we should expect to find in it helpful references to support our concerns and hopes and to cause us to know "God's plan" for us. We can take His word for that. There is power in praise and prayer, and we can feel that power by placing praise high in our prayer life. Finally we may get the habit and may occasionally even praise our brother and neighbor. Try it and see how tall he stands because of us.

If We Trust God, We Have Faith

Discontent can lead to murmuring—murmuring against His promise. Fear and doubt are not trusting. They counteract faith. If our fear and doubt deepens to terrible despair, haven't we said in effect, "I can't rely on You"? Aren't we saying, "Why do I have to do it all by myself?"

Counting Blessings Is Prayerful

If any justice remains in us, if any appreciation for all of the beauty and good, any sense of the love and peace we find amid all the troubled turmoil which we see and hear about us—well, what's wrong with saying "Thanks!"?

We believe that our faith ought to be a relaxed relationship with God. We know He loves us and won't leave us to ourselves. He supports us. Through Word and Spirit He enables our spirit to be faithful and our prayer life to stay alive. He gives us the opportunity to love our brothers. But we shouldn't accept His gifts without a grateful heart.

Why not keep up a good nutrition level, a good exercise regimen, in nurturing our own spiritual health? And when blessings keep coming back a hundredfold, what's wrong with saying, "Thanks, Lord!"?

Retirement Preparation Exercises

- Decide on and list two "new neighbor" action goals for yourself.
- Make a list of Scriptural passages that apply to your faith.
- Find out how to reach someone less blessed than you.
- Write out—if it will help—pro and con lists of your fears, doubts, discontent; then also of faith and trust.
- Try writing out your own new personal prayer of thanksgiving.

CHAPTER 9

How Well Will You Adjust to Retirement?

There have been too many bland pronouncements about the wonders of retirement. How wonderful it all is! Great to have nothing urgent to do! Do as I please! Just sit around, loaf and rest, and watch the world go by!

And then there are those other warnings which suggest that retirement can turn sour right in your comfortable rocking chair. There are those who say they want to play it by ear, while others like to get it all organized so they can make the most of it when the time comes.

Retirement Is a Certain Reality

One important point to remember: You are going to be retired sometime. Most everyone reaches that point in life when he no longer works at his job and no longer brings home a regular paycheck. This is quite an adjustment in itself, you'll find. But many are doing it wonderfully well and happily. A few are still messed up.

As with so many things in life, our attitude is finally the deciding factor. How we respond to our own retirement will indeed make all the difference. Like the doctor says, "There *is* a life after retirement, but you have to go out and find the life you want and make it as good as you want it to be." If you expect to have a good attitude based on your life's positive habits and experience, your retirement should be just fine.

Don't Retire Mentally — Switch Careers

There's something wrong with the word "retirement" all by itself. It sounds like the end, like "who cares anymore?" It's true we retire from one job and from our life's major career effort. But it's also true that retirement needn't be such a frightful word if we view it as our greatest opportunity yet for having a brand-new, exciting, avocational interest and for making new discoveries. Look ahead toward making this part of your lives the best part. Make it work without resorting to the customary pressures. Leave behind all those old problems.

Can you make time work for you? Before you say yes, check yourself on how disciplined you are, on how self-propelled your habits are. It's this extra gift of time which can fill your days or choke them to death. The difference is in how you will adjust to enjoying free time and using it.

Chart Retirement Income Expectations

Much has been made about the importance of financial planning to minimize the surprises which come along to take the joy out of retirement living. We can expect to have less income. We will probably also need less money for retired living.

But it still takes income every month to pay for food and shelter and to provide for emergencies, including emergencies like sickness and prolonged ill health. On the other hand, there are also those other promising and unscheduled opportunities which offer us new chances.

Assess your financial situation and see that it is well-ordered so that what you need comes to you on a regular, monthly cost-of-living basis. Income should include Social Security, any pensions or annuities, earnings from investments or real estate property, or any other conversion of assets into income. These should be arranged so that you have a dependable monthly cash-flow for living.

Something to Get Up for Every Day

Some people retire a little too thoroughly. They think that when their company retires them they are finished with life. Therefore they may quit all activities and involvements. It's especially unwise to do too much changing too fast. You will now have more free time to give to these community causes. Therefore you'll find them more of a satisfaction. You are more needed than ever because of the wisdom of your years.

You will need these connections, these new friends and associates. Don't become a brooding hermit. If you are a husband who is entering this new time of life with your wife still with you, be a man, now more than ever. Live as excitedly as you like or can, but let her live her life too, both independently and with you.

This Time It's What You Want

We speak of second careers, of avocational interests. But not everyone feels compelled or qualified to make something new happen. Whether your new dream is just for the fun of it, for neighbors who need you, or for yourselves, remember it's yours to decide. To do or not to do —it's your choice.

Before you retire, it's a good idea to figure out what kind of self-improvement goals you want to set for yourselves. Consider the suggestions in the paragraphs that follow.

Why Not Become a New Person?

Why not choose one of those classes being held in the adult schools or continuing education centers where you live? Why not try one night a week or perhaps one afternoon?

On another day or evening (you're free now and therefore it can be almost anytime) meet and visit with old friends; have simple dinners together; play cards; or watch some interesting television programs. Or just talk! Go for rides; visit scenic places together. Keep these warm personal relationships alive—for their sake and yours. You have more time now to be more involved. This makes you more interesting too! It'll be good to have you around. You're going to be more relaxed and have more fun.

Renew the Dating Game— You Have Time

One noon, afternoon, or evening a week do something special with your spouse. Either one of you can suggest and arrange it. Go shopping to interesting places. Go out to lunch. Or go by yourselves for inexpensive and pleasant evenings out which might include a movie. Go to a concert. Visit museums for particular shows that interest one or both of you. Drive into the country and explore new roads which you seldom had time for until now. Go to a play. Sample eating out if you wish. It's fun if you "mix it up." Let some be cheapies and some more plush.

A couple of mornings a week go into your home workshop, studio, or home office. Disappear into your garage or basement and fix up a place that's fun to come to. Try some new projects. Make something useful or something that's fun—for yourself, for your spouse, or for some friend. Remember, if you make it and give it, it's twice the gift—once in the joy of creating and once in the giving.

On Sundays go to church. Afterward have family dinners with children or with friends. Visit someone who may not have been able to get to church.

Open New Worlds

Once in a while go to your library and browse through old or new things which interest you: magazines and books.

Stay current in business or in fields which relate to your life's experience or which interest you now in some new way. Use the reference department and other resources of your library to orient yourself toward brand-new ideas and activities.

Between times pay interested attention to the home in which you live. Do what you can to keep it up and keep it looking nice. Fuss with the garden if this pleases you. Take on some maintenance or servicing project, but don't go over your head into hard and technical work.

Keep Alive Your Personal Lives — Both of You

Occasionally join with old friends and associates at church or club meetings. It's pleasant and constructive to exchange views with other people.

Depending upon where you live and what is available, you may find it interesting to go fishing or hunting, or to become an involved spectator at other sporting events. And share this interest with a friend!

Always remain available to lend a hand to someone less well off than you in any of the ways you may be more favored — in health, in assets, in resourcefulness of any kind.

Make Big Plans — Then Upset Them Sometimes

Remain flexible! It's fine to have a schedule, but it's even more fun to violate it. That's probably one of the most enjoyable rewards you'll find in retirement — the reward of being free to do as you please more of the time. Enjoy that freedom!

Beware that all that leisure does not kill you by boring you to death. Let it serve your new dreams and new ambitions. If you fear that you may be bored or lonely, seek new things to do with new people. Boredom is a choice! It happens to all of us, but we don't need to "keep living" there. Move outside of yourself! You'll soon have trouble remembering what it was you were bored about.

New Time
for Old and Loving Family Folks

We've said often that renewed relationships can now be developed with old friends and relatives. Aging family members often sit quite alone. You may find them repetitive and self-concerned beyond what is pleasing, but even this can serve as a reminder to yourself. Bringing your loving presence in such visits is a kind of gift for them. Witnessing how they respond to their limited circumstances can be an encouragement, or a warning, to you. It may encourage you to get interested and remain involved.

Poets have often insisted that anticipation is half the joy of realization. This has been found true among retired people as well. Medical schools report that people who look forward to retirement and plan for it, enjoy it more. They often live a longer, more satisfying life.

We Become What We Think

A philosopher we admire has said that you should be careful about what you want and what you would like to be, because if you want it, you will make it happen. So be careful what you wish for, because you will probably find it coming to you. This same blessing—or if you choose to make yours a burden—comes to many with retirement. Like so much of life, retirement turns out to be about what we expect it to be.

Finally: Adjustment Is an Attitude

How will you adjust to retirement? Remember, you earned this extra bonus time of life. Rewards are not delivered in some special way, they must be collected in person—by you. Plan as far ahead and as well as you can to cheerfully collect your own retirement reward.

Retirement Preparation Exercises

- Schedule a few ways to harness time.
- List a few community connections to stay involved in.
- List neglected activities retirement can make possible now.
- Face boredom's possibility with a list of countermeasures.
- Make a list of all the ways you feel you earned retirement.

CHAPTER 10

Practice Makes Retirement More Perfect

Some of life's best vacations were the ones we planned most thoroughly for. Retirement may easily be life's longest vacation.

Some free-thinking spirits protest that some of their best times came spontaneously. True! But true also that they were ready for the experience by being spontaneous themselves! What were good times? Times when unexpected friends stopped by for renewing old-time relationships; times we took the left fork on a strange road and discovered charming new places we hadn't expected; times we popped popcorn, told old stories, and sang old songs together. Joys can happen, and you can plan to make sure they will happen.

Life's Longest Vacation Deserves Planning

But a vacation as lengthy as retirement does better with advance planning. Yes leave room within all that time to permit the spontaneous to happen. But 15 to 30 years of retirement living is too long a period to leave to chance.

Remember how it was when you were a child eager to go to school, to get a passing grade, to be promoted to a new grade, to advance to the head of your class or to that special place in it where your efforts and talents took you? And then in your career job came study, reading, and meetings. How many seminars, night school sessions, readings of trade literature, and union meeting attendances it took for you to advance from apprentice to master! All of life finds us preparing for the next step so that we may be prepared to turn it to our advantage.

Where's the School for Retirees?

And now comes retirement with little or no schooling for this long and unfamiliar career time where no one directs our activities.

It may either be gross human waste or just a serious societal oversight. It's unjust to dump all those hard workers off of life's busy bus onto unfamiliar streets in unfamiliar lands with little or no organized preparation.

This fact makes it all the more important that you seriously make it your business to see that your retirement can be as perfect as it ought.

Enlist your spouse so that you will both be involved — together. This is a time of new togetherness, and that often gets to be one of the unexpected problems about retirement. Make simple fun of the whole learning business of retirement preparation. Make a classmate of your spouse and ask for her help and guidance. Seek her interested advice and see that you plan for enjoying part of it together and part of it separately — as individuals. You should retain your personal independence, but there is also room in retirement for satisfying new collaboration.

Even Travel Takes Practice — Beforehand

Where will you go — to travel *or* to live? Have you checked out these places? Why not get at this delightful assignment years early? Go there! Try the life! But don't buy until both of you have made up your minds that this is best for both of you. We've cautioned often: Try retirement living as if you were already retired. Have you the spirit for this fantasy and festival approach to life? It gives you a chance to work out the bugs, as so many sensible people have found. There are surprises in retirement. Why not find out ahead of time what some of these surprises are?

Play "Let's Pretend" as Though Retired

If you move to some new region where most of the people you see are strangers, it's not a bad idea for one or both of you to take a part-time job. Do it for pay or as a volunteer in church or community affairs. Sharing opens new doors and makes new friends and creates new horizons.

Agree on Patient Good Humor — Promise and Do

If all that new togetherness is just too much for the two of you at first, consider if one of you should get a job. Maybe this time it's her turn for her sake *and* for the sake of both of you.

Experiment, adapt, and adjust the retirement budget you plan to retire on. Do it beforehand for fun—and experience. The reality comes soon enough, and you might as well be ready for this shrunken pot o' gold at the end of your life's rainbow.

Don't move! Don't make any move before you check it out—without commitment, without investment. Don't get locked in and find yourself unable to come back to stay among the "good old familiar," if that turns out to be your decision.

Try the Buddy System — It Works for Some

Why can't another near-retirement couple help with your retirement experimentation? Many couples do it pleasantly—on a kind of informal buddy system where both have somewhat the same circumstances, timetables, and interests. They do it as good friends having good fun looking around and rejecting most of the mistakes beforehand. Follow our lighthearted advice on this point: Save at least a few mistakes for next year or the year after that. And don't make all of your mistakes too fast and too finally.

Raise the level of your anticipation by reading and studying and by writing for informative literature about places you are interested in. Restudy and review the history of where you now live. These things are pleasures in themselves. They help add fascination and involved awareness.

It's a conservative approach, but it's becoming to people who are approaching retirement, to keep one foot on familiar ground; to arrange for some kind of partial paycheck; to test out where to live geographically and specifically in what kind of housing circumstance.

Take Inventory of Your Real Roots

Keep in close touch with friends and family to help assess how much they will be missed and how ready you are to cut all of your strings.

Retirement adds up to more time and to almost less of everything else. Be careful how fast you "retreat" from life and how far you move away from comfortable, familiar, and needed roles. You *aren't* washed up! You can be anything you decide you want to be, especially if you are sensible about your capabilities.

Avoid big investment gambles which can threaten and even ruin people.

Who Says You Can't Come Home Again?

If you make a mistake, remember you need not forever choke on it all by yourselves. Swallow your pride, your foolish, costly pride. Are you able to admit a mistake and to come back from failure? If you moved too far away to a wrong place or to a place that turned out wrong for you, consider coming back. And come back happily and

74

with self-esteem intact. Old friends will be glad to have you.

As they say in the investment business, cut your losses and let your gains run on. If you lost, cut out when you're sure; cut out and come back where your prospects have always been more assured.

Retirement: Your Living Theater

The point about "rehearsing for retirement," or practicing for its perfection beforehand, is a childlike approach. It may not attract everyone. But life's performances are all rehearsed for! They are practiced to the kind of perfection that makes them acceptable when they are presented. Why not enjoy sampling how retirement might be by going forward to see how good you can make it? Then when your golden days come and you wind your retirement watch, you'll know where your compass is leading you. There'll be great comfort for both of you in that. If you are traveling alone—as a career woman, a widowed person, or another single—all these things still pertain and often so much more applies.

Try Permitting Some Pleasant Foolishness

Remember to keep all this "practice makes perfect" business fun. Write a note to yourself to remind yourself that you're learning how to stay "alive." You're learning how to manage for yourself, to stay involved with life. You'll be so much more fun to have around. You'll wonder about all that fuss about retirement loneliness.

Friends tell us—friends who scouted around to find out where they wanted to be and what they wanted to do with all that rewarding free time—that they had so many things lined up and so many places to be and people to see. They had to keep a check on how much of all this life's biggest vacation they could afford to enjoy.

Give Something of Yourself—Back to Others

Welcome your retirement with open and expectant arms. Welcome it as a gift for a just life from a just God.

Just one final word about rewards. They are best when they are *shared.* Remember to share your retirement reward with those who are closest to you. If you have had a good life and have enjoyed a goodly share of life's blessings remember to give some of it back by giving some to others. Share yourself, your talent, your time, and your worth.

Welcome your retirement—and let it become life's happiest reward.

Retirement Preparation Exercises

- Check former lists to see how you are doing. Make changes.
- Make "His and Her" lists for joint spouse activities.
- List cost-of-living "Now and Then" as a guide to income needs.
- Budget necessary income cash flow monthly. How big a gap?
- List where you will live; its nature and location.

BOOKS:

REHEARSE BEFORE YOU RETIRE, 208-page, paper, by Retirement Research, P. O. Box 107, Appleton, WI 54911 (revised, expanded, second edition—1972) . . . by Elmer Otte, $2.50.

RETIREMENT REHEARSAL GUIDEBOOK, 156-page text and workbook, used by individuals, families, corporations, banks, and universities as the guiding preparation text—for actual preparation exercises. Published by Pictorial Publishers, Indianapolis—1971—and also available from: Retirement Research, P. O. Box 107, Appleton, WI 54911. . . . by Elmer Otte, $6.95.

THE RETIREMENT HANDBOOK: by Joseph C. Buckley, published by Harper & Row, 1971; Fourth Revised and Enlarged Edition by Henry Schmidt. A Complete Planning Guide To Your Future, $7.95.

RETIREMENT—A TIME TO LIVE ANEW by Harry W. Hepner, McGraw-Hill, 1969, $6.95.

RETIRE TO ACTION by Julietta K. Arthur, Abingdon Press, Nashville, 1969. A thorough exploration of volunteerism, of interest to goal-oriented mature people, $5.95.

MAKE THE REST OF YOUR LIFE THE BEST OF YOUR LIFE, by Henry Legler, Simon & Schuster, 1967, $5.95.

MAGAZINES:

Modern Maturity, membership periodical of American Association for Retired Persons; and National Retired Teachers Ass'n. P. O. Box 729, Long Beach, Calif. 90801. Annual membership—$2.00.

Dynamic Maturity, membership periodical of Action for Independent Maturity, pre-retirement age category; 1225 Connecticut Ave., NW, Washington, D. C. 20036. Annual membership—$3.00.

Retirement Living, 150 East 58th Street, New York, N. Y. 10022. Annual subscription—$6.00.

Aging, Department of Health, Education and Welfare, Washington, D. C. 20201.